EXPLORING WORLD CULTURES

Malaysia

Laura L. Sullivan

Cavendish
Square

New York

Published in 2019 by Cavendish Square Publishing, LLC
243 5th Avenue, Suite 136, New York, NY 10016

Copyright © 2019 by Cavendish Square Publishing, LLC

First Edition

Website: cavendishsq.com

This publication represents the opinions and views of the author based on his or her personal experience, knowledge, and research. The information in this book serves as a general guide only. The author and publisher have used their best efforts in preparing this book and disclaim liability rising directly or indirectly from the use and application of this book.

All websites were available and accurate when this book was sent to press.

Library of Congress Cataloging-in-Publication Data

Names: Sullivan, Laura L., 1974- author.
Title: Malaysia / Laura L. Sullivan.
Description: First edition. | New York : Cavendish Square, 2019. |
Series: Exploring world cultures | Includes bibliographical references and index.
Identifiers: LCCN 2018018900 (print) | LCCN 2018019208 (ebook) |
ISBN 9781502643452 (ebook) | ISBN 9781502643445 (library bound) | ISBN 9781502643421(pbk.) |
ISBN 9781502643438 (6 pack)
Subjects: LCSH: Malaysia--Juvenile literature.
Classification: LCC DS592.6 (ebook) | LCC DS592.6 .S85 2019 (print) |
DDC 959.5--dc23
LC record available at https://lccn.loc.gov/2018018900

Editorial Director: David McNamara
Editor: Lauren Miller
Copy Editor: Nathan Heidelberger
Associate Art Director: Alan Sliwinski
Designer: Christina Shults
Production Coordinator: Karol Szymczuk
Photo Research: J8 Media

The photographs in this book are used by permission and through the courtesy of:
Cover robertharding/Alamy Stock Photo; p. 5 Yongyuan Dai/iStock; p. 6 pavalena/Shutterstock.com; p. 7 Peter Adams/Photolibrary/Getty Images; p. 8 Photo 12/Universal Images Group/Getty Images; p. 10, 26 MOHD RASFAN/AFP/Getty Images; p. 12 Jonathan Drake/Bloomberg/Getty Images; p. 13 mozakim/iStock/Thinkstock; p. 14 alexmatamata/iStock/Thinkstock; p. 15 mazzzur/iStock/Thinkstock; p. 16 Uwe Aranas/CEphoto/Wikimedia Commons/File:Sabah Malaysia Welcoming-Contingent Hari-Merdeka-2013-17.jpg/CC BY-SA 3.0; p. 18 anythings/Shutterstock.com; p. 19 Papa Annur/Shutterstock.com; p. 20 Niro5/Wikimedia Commons/File:Masjid Negara KL.jpg/CC BY-SA 2.5; p. 21 Mohd Samsul Mohd Said/Getty Images; p. 22 mtcurado/iStock; p. 24 laughingmango/iStock; p. 27 ADEK BERRY/AFP/Getty Images; p. 28 dolphfyn/Shutterstock.com.

Printed in the United States of America

Contents

Introduction

Malaysia's national motto is "Unity Is Strength." It is perfect for this diverse and beautiful country. Malaysia is located in Southeast Asia. Many people have ruled Malaysia. Malaysia has influences from countries like China, Thailand, and India.

Malaysia is growing fast. It has large cities and new technology. However, it also has a lot of traditions.

Malaysia is a popular place to visit. There are beautiful beaches and coral reefs. There are also rain forests and cool animals. Malaysian people enjoy sports like soccer and badminton. Music and dance are important too.

Malaysia has delicious foods, fun activities, and special celebrations. It is a fascinating place to explore.

Kuala Lumpur is Malaysia's capital.

Geography

Malaysia is a country in Southeast Asia. It is made up of two areas, East Malaysia and West Malaysia. The South China

Malaysia is located in Southeast Asia.

Sea separates them. East Malaysia is part of the island of Borneo. West Malaysia is about 400 miles (640 kilometers) away. It borders Thailand.

Malaysia is not a big country, but it has a lot of coastline. In fact, it has the twenty-ninth longest

FACT!

The island of Borneo is shared by three countries: Brunei, Malaysia, and Indonesia.

A Country of Caves

The Mulu Caves are one of the largest cave systems in the world. They are found in Gunung Mulu National Park on the island of Borneo.

coastline of any country in the world. Many small islands belong to Malaysia.

Both parts of Malaysia have mountains. The land is hot and humid. **Monsoons**, or times of very heavy rain, happen in two long cycles each year. Malaysia has rain forests. Lots of plants and animals live there.

Malaysia has many rain forests.

People first lived in Malaysia forty thousand years ago. Eventually, traders from India and China visited. They brought new religions, arts, and ideas.

Over time, parts of Malaysia belonged

Tunku Abdul Rahman led Malaysia after it gained independence.

FACT!

Tunku Abdul Rahman was the first prime minister after Malaysia became independent. His nickname is "Bapa Malaysia," or "Father of Malaysia."

to different empires. Then, in the 1500s, a few European countries took over parts of Malaysia. Portugal, the Netherlands, and Britain moved in at different times. They gave the area different names.

The Japanese invaded Malaysia in World War II. After the Japanese left, there was an independence movement. In 1963, Malaysia was formed and became independent. It included Singapore, but later Singapore became its own country. For a time, the different **ethnic groups** fought. However, when the economy started improving, race relations also improved.

Indian Storytelling

Malaysia is mentioned in the Indian epic the Ramayana. It was called the "Golden Peninsula" for its wealth and gold mines.

9

VOTE ✓

Malaysia is a constitutional **monarchy**. Thirteen states make up Malaysia. Nine of these states have a royal family. The other four have a governor. Every five years, a new king is elected from Malaysia's nine royal families.

Muhammad V of Kelantan became king in 2016.

The king does not have much power. Instead, a person called a prime minister leads

FACT!

The Royal Malaysia Police are in charge of law enforcement.

The constitution of Malaysia governs the whole country. Each individual Malaysian state has its own laws too.

Malaysia. The prime minister is head of the executive branch of government. There is also a **parliament**. It makes up the legislative branch. Lastly, there is a court system that makes up the judicial branch.

Kuala Lumpur is Malaysia's capital and its biggest city. The king lives there. However, the prime minister and **cabinet** live and work in the city of Putrajaya. This is because Kuala Lumpur was too crowded.

Malaysia's economy is strong. Farmers grow crops like rice and cocoa. They also grow oil palm trees. These trees make palm oil. Malaysia's natural resources, like petroleum and tin, are sold around

Malaysians make electronics that are sold in other countries.

the world. Factories in Malaysia make things like electronics and medical technology.

FACT!

Malaysia is the world leader in Islamic banking. This means that banks and their customers follow the rules of Islam.

The Uses of Palm Oil

Palm oil is used for many things. It is used for cooking, to make candles, and even to make medicine.

Malaysia's economy is the third biggest in Southeast Asia. Its currency is the **ringgit**. One US dollar was the same value as 3.88 ringgits as of January 2018.

Malaysian ringgits are very colorful.

Tourism is growing quickly in Malaysia. People like to visit the country's beautiful natural sights. Others come as medical tourists. This means they come to see Malaysian doctors. Operations are cheaper in Malaysia than in their home country.

13

Much of Malaysia is covered in tropical rain forests. Some of the forests are 130 million years old. Many animals live there. Native animals include tigers, leopards, orangutans, elephants, and cobras.

The Malayan tiger is a rare and protected animal.

Malaysia is home to at least 20 percent of the

FACT!

The Malaysian rafflesia plant has the biggest flowers in the world. They grow up to 3 feet, 3 inches (1 meter) across.

entire world's plant and animal species!

Today, Malaysia has more laws that protect the environment. However, some activities hurt parts of Malaysia. Logging is one activity hurting Malaysia's forests.

The record-breaking rafflesia plant has the world's biggest flowers.

A Place for Plants and Animals

Malaysia is a **megadiverse** country. This means there is a very large number of native plants and animals. Only seventeen countries in the world are like this.

Malaysia has more than thirty-one million people. Its population is growing.

The Malaysian people come from many different ethnic groups and cultures.

Malaysian traditional clothes are diverse and colorful.

The largest group are called **bumiputera**. It means "sons of the soil." They are native Malaysians

FACT!

People in Malaysia live for an average of seventy-five years. In the United States, it is eighty years.

Malaysian Families

Most Malaysian families have two children. On average, *bumiputera* families have more children than Chinese or Indian Malaysian families.

who follow traditional Malaysian culture and are Muslim. They are given special privileges. These include discounts on housing and better schools for their children.

Chinese Malaysians are another ethnic group. They make up about 20 percent of the population. Malaysian Indians make up about 6 percent of people. Many ethnic groups that live in Malaysia today first came there as workers when the British were in charge.

17

Lifestyle

Family, respect, and courtesy are important to Malaysian people. Home life varies depending on the ethnic group.

Malaysian Islamic women usually wear a *tudong* in public.

Most Islamic Malaysians follow Islamic law and traditions at home. Men can have more than one wife. However, this is not common in big cities. A husband must care for his wife and children. A wife must obey her husband.

FACT!

Malaysians use their right hand to shake hands, give gifts, and eat. The left hand is used for cleaning the body.

Children start school at age six and finish high school at age eighteen. Many Malaysian students then go to college. In 2016, more female students (48 percent) went to college than male students (40 percent).

Children study Malaysian and English in school.

Malaysian women are well educated. Around 47 percent of Malaysian women have jobs.

Respecting Elders

The elderly are held in the highest respect. When they talk, the whole room listens. Younger people often lower their heads when they walk by an elderly person.

Religion

Many religions are practiced in Malaysia. Most native Malaysians are Muslim. Most Chinese Malaysians are Buddhist. Most Indian Malaysians are Hindu. Some people also practice Christianity, Taoism, and Confucianism.

The Masjid Negara is the national mosque of Malaysia.

Malaysia is secular. This means that laws are not based on religion. However, Islam is the official religion. In some states, there are sharia

All Muslim children in public school have to take Islamic studies. All non-Muslim students take a morals and ethics class.

Holidays and Religion

National holidays cover many religions. Among them are the Prophet Muhammad's birthday (Islam), Christmas (Christianity), and Dewali (Hinduism).

Dewali is the Hindu festival of lights.

courts that govern only Muslims. They handle religious problems for things like marriage, divorce, and inheritance.

Though Malaysia is secular, there are laws that restrict Muslims. For example, Muslims cannot join another religion. However, people following other religions can choose to follow Islam. Also, a Muslim cannot marry a non-Muslim person unless they agree to follow Islam.

21

Language

Malaysian is the official
language of Malaysia.
It is also called Bahasa
Malaysia, or Bahasa
Melayu. It can be written
in a traditional style
called Jawi. It looks
similar to Arabic. Often,
Malaysian is written in the same alphabet
as English.

This sign is written in
Malaysian and English.

Some Malaysians are related to early Spanish
or Portuguese colonists. They speak versions
of Spanish or Portuguese.

English is widely spoken. It is taught in all schools. Some regions even recognize it as their official second language.

There is also a hybrid language called Manglish. It combines English, Malaysian, Chinese, and other languages. It is one way for people who speak different languages to communicate.

Many Languages

Most people speak Malaysian or English, but there are 137 languages spoken in Malaysia. In East Malaysia, most of the native tribes have their own languages. These languages are related to Malaysian.

Traditional Malaysian art includes baskets and woven wall rugs called tapestries. In Islam, art should not show people or animals. Instead, artists use patterns or images of plants.

There are large street festivals to celebrate Chinese New Year.

Dance and acting are important to Malaysian culture. A type of theater called *mak yong* includes both. *Dikir barat* is a popular style of dance. It

FACT!

Hari Merdeka, Malaysian Independence Day, is celebrated on August 31.

24

The Art of *Silat*

Silat is a martial art from Malaysia. It is often set to music and performed at royal events or weddings.

combines poetic singing with movement. It usually includes drums or hand clapping. There are *dikir barat* competitions.

One of the biggest holidays in Malaysia is Eid al-Fitr. It celebrates the end of Ramadan, a Muslim holy month. There are feasts, singing, and dancing. Chinese New Year is another important celebration. It lasts for fifteen days. Festivities include parades and fireworks.

Malaysians enjoy playing and watching many sports. Some favorite sports are soccer, field hockey, and badminton.

Wau bulan kites are big and beautiful.

Kite flying is a very popular hobby. The kites, called *wau bulan*, are huge and brightly colored. They can fly more than 1,500 feet (457 m) high. *Wau bulan* kites are one of Malaysia's national symbols.

Malaysia has won several Olympic medals. Seven were silver. Most were for badminton.

A Traditional Malaysian Sport

Sepak takraw is a game that is similar to volleyball, but with one big difference. Players hit a ball over a net using only their feet, legs, and chests—no hands.

In *sepak takraw*, players pass a ball over a net without using their hands.

With so much coastline, water sports are also very popular. Many people enjoy boating and swimming. Both tourists and natives scuba dive in the beautiful reefs.

Food

Nasi lemak is the national dish of Malaysia.

Malaysian food has changed over time. Neighbors like Thailand, India, and China introduced Malaysians to new spices and recipes. Today, each region in Malaysia has special dishes and flavors.

Rice makes up most Malaysian meals. *Nasi lemak* is the national dish of Malaysia. It is made by steaming rice in coconut milk and then adding spices. Many dishes have chili peppers. They can be spicy or sweet. Another common ingredient is shrimp paste.

FACT!

Mooncakes are pastries stuffed with bean or lotus-seed paste. Chinese Malaysians eat them during the Moon Festival. It is also called the Mid-Autumn Festival. It happens every September or October.

Seafood and poultry are common. For religious reasons, Muslims do not eat pork and Hindus do not eat beef. Tropical fruits like rambutans and mangosteens are popular.

Cooking with Palm Trees

All parts of the coconut palm are used in Malaysian cooking. Some foods are even cooked in coconut palm leaves.

Glossary

bumiputera   Malaysians of Malay origin who practice Islam.

cabinet   A group of advisors to the leader of a country.

ethnic group   People who share a common background or culture.

megadiverse   Having an unusually large number of animal and plant species.

monarchy   The kind of government led by a king or queen.

monsoon   A seasonal system of heavy rain.

parliament   A group of people in a government who are chosen to make a country's laws.

ringgit   The Malaysian currency (money).

Find Out More

Books

Barnard, Bryn. *The Genius of Islam: How Muslims Made the Modern World*. New York: Knopf, 2011.

Lyons, Kay. *Malaysian Children's Favorite Stories*. Rutland, VT: Tuttle Publishing, 2014.

Website

Ducksters: Malaysia

http://www.ducksters.com/geography/country.

php?country=Malaysia

Video

Malaysia: Learn About Asian Countries for Kids

https://www.youtube.com/watch?v=BHUWCqEu-Us

Index

About the Author

Laura L. Sullivan is the author of more than forty fiction and nonfiction books for children and young adults, including the fantasies *Under the Green Hill* and *Guardian of the Green Hill*. She lives in Florida, where she likes to bike, hike, kayak, hunt fossils, and practice Brazilian jiujitsu.